My Homework Ate

MW01614446

Cartoon Basics for the Successful Educator

Edited by Carol Bucheri and Delaine McCullough

Phi Delta Kappa International
Bloomington, Indiana, U.S.A.

Cover cartoon by Scott Arthur Masear

Published by Phi Delta Kappa International
408 North Union Street
P.O. Box 789
Bloomington, Indiana 47402-0789
U.S.A.

Copyright © 2005 by Phi Delta Kappa International

All rights reserved
Unauthorized use of any material herein is strictly prohibited.

Library of Congress Catalog Card Number 2005927946

ISBN 0-87367-858-3

Printed in the United States of America

Foreword

Four pairs of shoes, a Sony Discman along with assorted CDs and cases, pine cones, various holiday gift wrappings, a box of chocolates, and most of a two-pound bag of confectioner's sugar — sounds like a midwinter shopping list, doesn't it? Now throw in an array of rocks, a half-dozen bottles of vitamins, the lens cap from a camera, a pair of prescription glasses, several unmatched socks, and a few issues of the *New Yorker*. Is the picture getting any clearer?

Since the day we sprang our dog "Buddy" from the pen at the local humane society, he's been eating his way through our household and straight into our hearts (not to mention the savings account). With a cock of the head and a melting glance, he clearly communicates that he was, after all, only looking for a little midday snack. Principals and teachers are no doubt familiar with a similar combination of exasperating misconduct and heartbreaking charm, which their students have raised to an art form. As you will discover in the following pages, that art form frequently turns out to be a cartoon, and our aggravations quickly dissolve into laughter.

Thanks to the abundant talents of the cartoonists whose work is collected here, the *Phi Delta Kappan* is able to offer its readers the luxury of bypassing the aggravation and simply laughing knowingly at the antics and foibles of a recognizable assortment of miscreants. This anthology of cartoons culled from the past several years of the journal concludes with brief biographies of the cartoonists. The *Kappan* staff can affirm that Martha Campbell, Scott Arthur Masear, and Dave Carpenter, to name a few, are a joy to work with. Their diverting characters are guaranteed to provide amusement, even during the most stressful of days. Enjoy these great cartoons — but, please, try to keep this book out of the reach of your canine buddies.

— *Carol Bucheri, Bloomington, Indiana*

Bon Appétit

*The successful educator knows that proper nutrition
is essential to school achievement.*

"*My brother ate my homework.*"

"The only difference between you and me, Flanders,
is that I read the homework before I ate it."

"*I wish he'd do his homework earlier. I hate eating this late.*"

"You always go that extra mile, don't you, Monica?"

Dogs had it rough in the days when homework was done on sun-baked clay tablets.

"*I can't decide between the English essay and the math problems.*"

"Too much beanie and not enough weenie."

"*What's the 'catch of the day'?*"

"The bog ate my homework."

"She's our spell checker."

"Sorry I'm late. I heard a can opening."

"I guess you'll be glad when I learn to read."

The Arts and Sciences

The successful educator knows that exposure to a broad curriculum enhances learning.

"Thank you, Susan. I must say — that's the most unusual rendition of 'The Raven' that I've ever heard."

"Larry says it's his 'extended' family."

"*Cheer up, Robert, maybe something will grow by morning. If not, we can write down one result — don't wait until the night before your science project is due.*"

10/2001

"*Surely you can get this information online.*"

"I don't think you're a bad artist, honey. Why do you say that?"

"*Periodically, he breaks into interpretive dance so his right brain doesn't atrophy.*"

"Oops!"

11/2002

"I can't believe he won first prize with the same exhibit as last year!"

"*Wait, Harold! I'm getting a bad feeling about this.*"

"*Barry's drawing — his mother is a dentist.*"

"No, Carl, 'creative writing' does not mean you may write your report in a language you've made up."

4/2001

"Just turn in your report and get back with the others, Adam!"

Principal and Teacher

*The successful educator relies on colleagues
for professional and emotional support.*

"Mr. Clark isn't in today. He called in sick of the whole thing."

"*Since reorganizing the schedule, we haven't figured out what to do with Harris.*"

"*My doctor limits me to one cup of coffee a day.*"

"*Stunt double!*"

"What I did on my sabbatical."

"*Good. Then there's no reason to grade all those papers tonight.*"

*"Things to bring up at the next school board meeting.
First . . . the need for more office space."*

The Intelligence Report

The successful educator picks up valuable tips about classroom management from more experienced colleagues.

"I had this installed to help our absentee problems, Ms. Barnes."

"*And I would appreciate it if all of you kept your eyes on your own work.*"

"For the last time, Billy . . . you can visit the rest room when the lesson is over!"

"*This happens every time we read about Curious George.*"

"*Now that I have your attention, class . . .*"

"*Just be sure you have someone in each outfit.*"

"That's all for today, children. We'll have to finish with our tardy excuses tomorrow."

"*Ms. Henson, you're going in for Ms. Bleckmore.*"

"Maybe next time you'll listen when I tell you not to lean back in your chair, Jimmy!"

4/1998

"*Well, if they asked me to come up with a substitute for a teacher, another teacher would be the last thing on my list.*"

"*Let me know if there's anything else your regular teacher does.*"

"*Well, look who decided to honor us with his presence.*"

"*Aren't there enough problems in the world already?*"

Family Circle

The successful educator knows that parent involvement is vital to school success.

"School starts tomorrow, doesn't it, Mom?"

"I considered home schooling, but then I realized they'd be home all day."

"If your friends told you to fly into a windshield, would you do that, too?"

"*This is my seatmate, Billy. We worked with glue today.*"

"My name was David, but that sounded old-fashioned, so I changed it to DVD."

12/2000

"*I'm tired of breaking up fights between you two! What do I look like? A referee?*"

"*Did I have a rough childhood?*"

"No, I'm not in favor of home schooling."

"*Mom. Dad. I think your expectations may be a little too high.*"

"*A thesaurus! I happen to know a little about dinosaurs, myself.*"

"My parents are trying to wean me off instant gratification."

"The amazing thing is, he's never seen a Jackson Pollock!"

"Boy, if you think nobody cares about you, try forgetting
your homework three days in a row!"

"I can't figure it out . . . we had a substitute teacher, but she looked real to me!"

"Mom says she'll come to the PTA meeting if you'll come to her Tupperware party."

Shanks

9/1998

"Mom, you know that dream you have where you're at school and you're having a test and you don't know any of the answers? Well, that happened to me today in real life."

3/1999

A Child's Life

The successful educator knows that each child brings a unique set of gifts and talents to the school community.

"I don't understand this. I got half of the answers right on this math test, and the teacher only gave me 50%."

"*I think I need help. I'm hooked on phonics.*"

"*What do you mean, you're having trouble relating to the subject?*
This is an autobiography, Kim — you are the subject."

"Turns out Joan of Arc wasn't Noah's wife."

"*When do we get our tattoos?*"

"*I would've done better on that test if I'd come to school with my calculator instead of the remote control.*"

"Man, that test didn't go so well at all — I stopped to think and couldn't get started again."

"*We brainstormed.*"

"*He has to write an essay without using the words 'cool,' 'like,' or 'awesome.'*"

"Here's my 'What I Did This Summer' report. However, there were a
few minutes I couldn't account for."

"Please tell me I'm having one of those dreams where I show up at school in my underwear."

"They must really think we're slow readers. They gave us all summer to read this list, and I read it on the way down the hall."

Off the Wall

The successful educator knows that creativity
should be nurtured and encouraged.

"I have this fantasy of being the director of the nursing home
you'll eventually be sent to."

"*Just give me your tardy excuse without the Greek chorus, Anthony.*"

"The teacher said I was trying today. Very trying."

"If your teacher ever asks, 'Do I look stupid to you?' do not say yes!"

"I can't come to school today because I have a barking cough. Wanna hear it?"

"When your teacher scolds you, you should never, ever say, 'Quack, quack, water off a duck's back.'"

"*Then I said to Ms. Rand, 'Do you mind? I'm on the phone.'*"

"*Why did I miss school yesterday? I'll be honest,
Ms. O'Donnell, I didn't really miss it.*"

"But I do have my act together — that was it, back there in your room."

"Ms. Storlie, my computer crashed."

"Billy can't come to school because he has a stomachache? Wow!"

"*You told me not to bring home another bad report card, so I left it at school.*"

"*If he's such a genius, how come he couldn't talk his parents out of violin lessons?*"

"*That's the last time I tell Johnny Patrick to clean out his desk.*"

"*Mom, Jason said I'm not the hope for our nation's future.*"

"Can I call you back? This isn't a good time."

Travel and Leisure

The successful educator knows that experiences beyond the classroom door are important to the development of well-rounded children.

"When I approved your field trip, Ms. Harris, I assumed you'd be going along with your class."

The first fifth-grade field trip to Mars gets off to a rough start.

"What would happen if you were scared half to death twice?"

"*I think he's taken too many rubber bands to the back of the head.*"

"Having a bad hat day?"

"We were out of the house before I remembered I needed something
for the valentine party today."

9/1999

"Can I have your number in case I start liking girls?"

"Stop sniffing lunches."

"*Then on the matter of the new school buses, that's four ayes and one I-had-to-walk-two-miles-to-school-through-a-foot-of-snow-when-I-was-young.*"

"*Honey, e-mail Bobby and tell him dinner's ready.*"

"*What's the big deal? We've been online for a hundred years.*"

Milestones

The successful educator takes time to celebrate students' successes and help them learn from their challenges.

Bill missed rehearsal.

"Please, Mother, not yet!"

The Cartoonists

George Abbott

A retired postal worker, George Abbott has been cartooning for several years. His wife Marianne helps prepare cartoons for mailing and offers advice and encouragement. Abbott's first big sale was to the *National Enquirer*; since then, his cartoons have appeared in most major magazines and in many trade journals, as well as in several collections. "I do a few, I sell a few," he says. Since retirement he divides his time between cartooning and model railroading.

Charles Almon

Charles Almon received an M.F.A. from Pratt Institute, majoring in painting, after some years as a corporate art director (abstract expressionism had peaked).

Glenn Bernhardt

Glenn Bernhardt has contributed to virtually every publication of significance that features freelance "gag" cartoons — and he has outlasted many of them. (He does not consider his work responsible for their demise.)

Currently, *Good Housekeeping*, the *National Enquirer* (which has never been sued over one of his cartoons), and the *Wall Street Journal* are on his client list.

Bernhardt lives with his wife Mary Lou in Carmel, California, where they spend time directing tourists to Clint Eastwood's house.

Art Bouthillier

Art Bouthillier is a freelance cartoonist whose work may appear in as many as 150 different publications at any give time. Some of the magazines he frequently contributes to are *Better Homes & Gardens*, the *Saturday Evening Post*, and *Good Housekeeping*.

Bouthillier is also the editorial cartoonist for his local newspaper, the *South Whidbey Record*, for which he won the 1989 Excellence in Journalism award for cartooning and illustration, and is a recipient of the Golden Toonie award from Cartoonists Northwest.

Martha Campbell

With a B.F.A. from Washington University,

St. Louis, Martha Campbell is a former writer/designer for Hallmark Cards. A freelance cartoonist since 1973, she started when her daughter was 3, she was expecting her second child (a son), and her studio was a closet just wide enough for a drawing board. Now her children are college graduates, and her studio is a full-sized room with a copier, a computer, four file cabinets, and a dog. She lives in Harrison, Arkansas, with the same husband she started out with — and, of course, neither of them has changed at all.

Dave Carpenter

Dave Carpenter started cartooning professionally in 1976, becoming a full-time cartoonist in 1981. Along with *Phi Delta Kappan*, Dave's cartoons can also be found in *Harvard Business Review*, *Reader's Digest*, *Barron's*, the *Wall Street Journal*, and *Good Housekeeping* as well as other publications. Having had a brief stint at teaching junior high art, he appreciates and salutes all teachers.

Benita Epstein

Benita Epstein's cartoons appear in hundreds of publications including the *New Yorker*, *Barron's*, the *Wall St. Journal*, *Harvard Business Review*, *Chicken Soup for the Soul* books, greeting cards, and three of her own cartoon collections. Her newspaper panel, *Drawing a Crowd*, was syndicated, and a daily cartoon ran on Verizon cell phones. She has five division nominations from the National Cartoonists Society.

James Estes

A full-time cartoonist for more than 35 years, Estes numbers among his clients *Woman's World*, *Boys' Life*, *Good Housekeeping*, *Mature Living*, *Highlights for Children*, and *Ebony*. He and wife Martha, who've been married for 41 years, obviously stressed the importance of education to their children. Son Robert is a West Point graduate, daughter Kelley is completing her Ph.D. and working as a diagnostician in a high school, and daughter Paige is completing her eighth year teaching music and physical education at the primary level. The Esteses also have five grandchildren.

Randy Glasbergen

More than 20,000 of Randy Glasbergen's cartoons have been published by America Online, *The Funny Times*, *Glamour*, the *Wall Street Journal*, and many others. His comic panel, "The Better Half," is syndicated worldwide by King Features Syndicate. Randy is also the author of several books, including *Technology Bytes!*, *Are We Dysfunctional Yet?*, *Attack of the Zit Monster and Other Teenage Terrors*, *How to Be a Successful Cartoonist*, and *Getting Started Drawing and Selling Cartoons*. He also creates "Today's Cartoon by Randy Glasbergen," which appears exclusively on the Web at www.glasbergen.com. Randy lives in New York State with his family, a bloated poodle, and several deeply troubled cats.